I Am Not a
BOX!

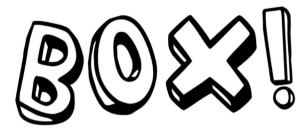

by Emily Kington

HUNGRY
TOMATO™

MINNEAPOLIS

Contents

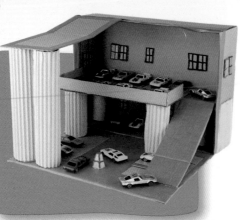
You will need a grown-up to help you make these fantastic models.

Ready to have fun...

Recycling unwanted things into art is really fun, and it doesn't cost a fortune—all the main ingredients were going to be thrown away!

Don't throw away leftover boxes and cardboard. Use them to make art, and you will soon have your very own art collection.

See page 24 for more information about materials.

You will need...

Boxes	Egg carton
Paper	Tinfoil
Craft glue	Bottle caps
Pipe cleaners	Metal pieces
Cardboard	Craft sticks
Beads or buttons	Milk carton
Tissue paper	Cork
Cotton balls	Acrylic paint
String	Paintbrush
Masking tape	Markers
	Sponge

Monster Money- Eating Bank

This friendly, hairy money monster looks hungry, but it's a perfect place to hide your hard-earned cash.

You will need...

Tissue box
Paper
Cardboard
Egg carton
String
Pipe cleaners
Craft glue
Sponge
Acrylic paint
Paintbrush
Masking tape

You are ready to become a monstrously good saver!

Monster Money-Eating Bank

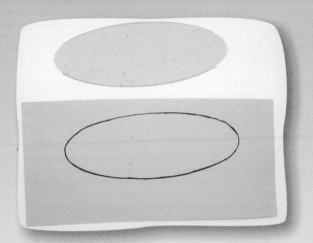

1 **Remove** the opening flap from the tissue box and draw around the shape onto paper.

2 Draw some teeth.

Cut your drawing in half, then cut out the top and bottom sets of teeth. Leave some space for some glue.

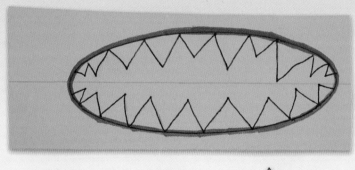

3 **Glue** the teeth to the inside of the box.

4 Make a monster tongue from paper.

5 Cut one pod from the bottom of an egg carton and cut it in half to make two monster eyelids.

Cut out ten disks from cardboard, five for each eye. Glue the disks together in a stack and paint. Then glue the eyes to the egg carton eyelids.

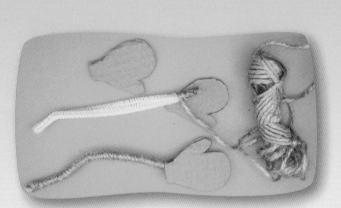

6 Wind string around two pipe cleaners for the monster arms.

Cut out four hands.

Sandwich one end of the pipe cleaner between two hands and glue together.

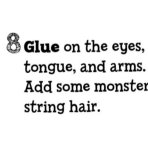

7 Paint your box. A sponge dabbed in paint works well.

8 Glue on the eyes, tongue, and arms. Add some monster string hair.

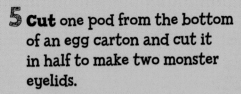

Recycled Robot Mechanic

This is a great project for a rainy day. You can design your robot any way you want.

This little robot is a

very smart mechanic!

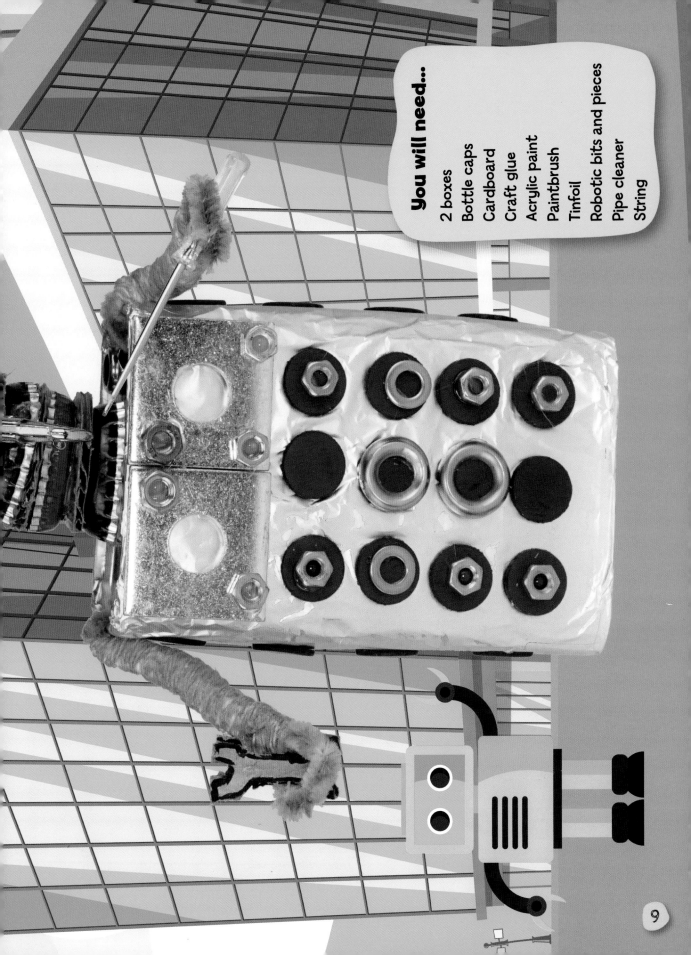

You will need...

2 boxes
Bottle caps
Cardboard
Craft glue
Acrylic paint
Paintbrush
Tinfoil
Robotic bits and pieces
Pipe cleaner
String

Recycled Robot Mechanic

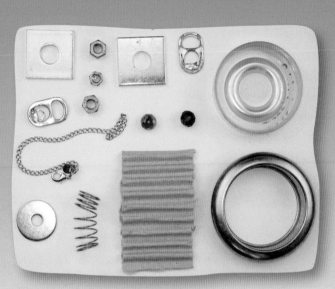

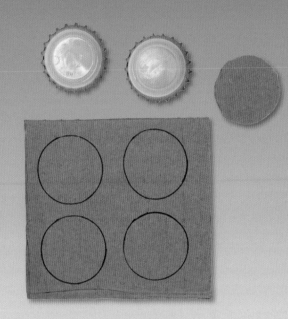

1 **Search** your junk drawer for robotic-looking bits and pieces.

2 **Cut out** some disks from cardboard. They should be about the same size as your bottle caps.

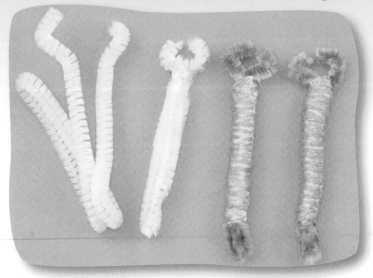

3 **Glue** the bottle caps and disks together in a stack to make the robot's neck.

4 **Make** some robot arms by folding pipe cleaners in half. winding string around them, and painting them gray.

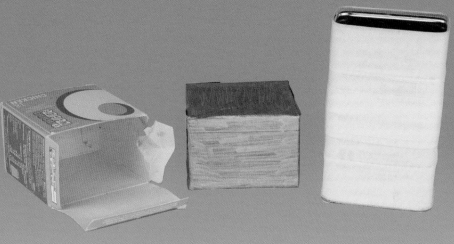

5 Find boxes for the head and body. You can cover them in masking tape and paint them, or you can cover them in tinfoil.

6 Glue the neck to the head.

Use nuts, beads, and bottle caps to make the robot's face.

Make the robot some tools.

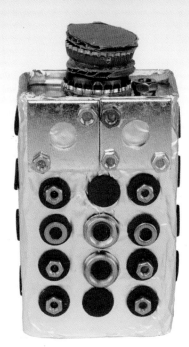

7 Cover the body in tinfoil. Add some bits and pieces to make it look robotic.

8 Glue the head and arms onto the body.

Woodland Theater

You could use fairy lights for special effects. Good luck with the performance!

Create your very own theater and perform plays starring the woodland creatures you make.

You will need...

Box lid or box
Paper
Craft sticks
Beads
Painted twigs
Tissue paper
Masking tape
Craft glue
Acrylic paint
Paintbrush
Pipe cleaners
Cotton ball
Wooden skewer

Woodland Theater

1 Ask an adult to cut out the middle of the lid and the bottom portion as shown. Make a hole for the skewer.

If your box is shiny, cover it in masking tape so that you can paint it.

2 Draw a scene on a piece of paper and cut it out.

3 Paint the outside of your box. Glue the scenery to the inside.

Use tissue paper for the curtains and add some painted twigs for decoration.

4 Decide what characters you would like to star in the show.

Draw them onto paper, color them in, and cut them out.

Cotton balls make great fluffy tails.

5 Glue them onto craft sticks. Add some beads to make the eyes.

Use a pipe cleaner for a curly tail.

Draw feet onto the craft stick.

6 Position the theater on the edge of a table. Tape it in place using masking tape.

Now it's time to start the show!

Decorative Birdhouse Light

This is a simple thing to make during the holidays. Add it to your decorations... it's recycling at its best!

You will need...

Milk carton
Masking tape
Cork
Paper
Cardboard
String
Craft glue
Acrylic paint
Paintbrush
Battery-operated fairy lights (optional)

Make your own little piece of holiday art.

Decorative Birdhouse Light

1 Clean the milk carton thoroughly and ask an adult to remove the spout.

Cover the waxy surface in masking tape so it is ready to paint.

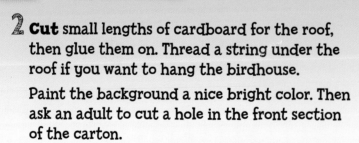

2 Cut small lengths of cardboard for the roof, then glue them on. Thread a string under the roof if you want to hang the birdhouse.

Paint the background a nice bright color. Then ask an adult to cut a hole in the front section of the carton.

3 Draw some decorative birds onto paper. Glue them into place.

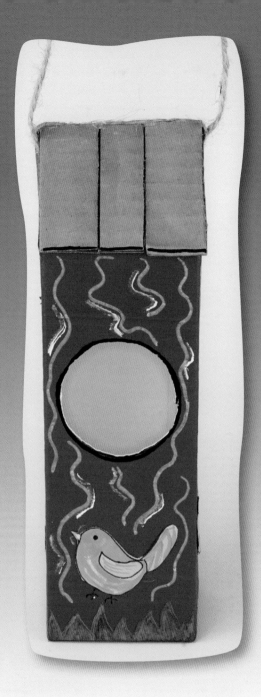

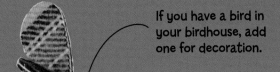
If you have a bird in your birdhouse, add one for decoration.

4 **Finish** decorating the birdhouse. Add some fairy lights if you have them.

5 **Glue** a cork under the hole to make a nice perch.

Parking Garage

Car enthusiasts will love building this parking garage. It can be up and running in no time at all, and you don't even need paint!

You will need...

Cardboard boxes

Colored masking tape

Large and small paper rolls

Egg carton

Craft glue

Marker

Corrugated cardboard (optional)

Bring in the cars.
Parking is free, and there
is plenty of room.

Parking Garage

1 **Ask** an adult to help you cut the front of your box open. Use masking tape to cover the edges.

Make a ramp out of cardboard and cover it with tape.

Measure the width left after allowing for the ramp and make the upper level of the parking garage.

2 **Cover** the paper rolls in corrugated cardboard.

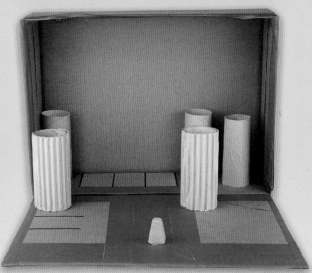

3 **Stick** down masking tape for the road and use a ruler and marker to mark out parking spaces.

Glue on small paper rolls to support the upper level and make a post from part of an egg carton.

4 **Glue** the ramp and second level into place on top of the paper rolls. Add a safety barrier so the cars can't fall off!

Glue on large paper rolls and make an outside roof to fit. Cover the edges with tape.

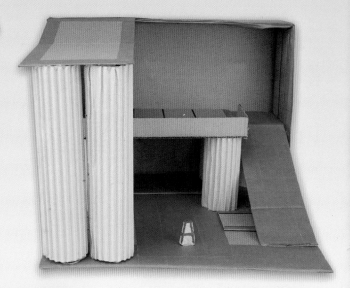

5 **Make** some windows for the garage.

Useful items

3 water jars for cleaning brushes while painting.

Scissors

Ruler

Picture Credits

(abbreviations: t = top; b = bottom; m = middle; l = left; r = right; bg = background)

Shutterstock:
Chereliss 13tr; Darya Palchikova 4bl; ideyweb 17bl; Ihor Biliavskyi 3bg & 12bg; MicroOne 4bg; Moiseenko Liubov 20bg; Rimma Z 20bl; SlaSla 16bg; SlyBrowney 12br; Vectorpocket 8bg; VectorSun 9br.

Original edition copyright 2019 by Hungry Tomato Ltd.
Copyright © 2019 by Lerner Publishing Group, Inc.

Hungry Tomato® is a trademark of Lerner Publishing Group

All rights reserved. International copyright secured. No part of this book may be reproduced, stored in a retrieval system, or transmitted in any form or by any means—electronic, mechanical, photocopying, recording, or otherwise—without the prior written permission of Lerner Publishing Group, Inc., except for the inclusion of brief quotations in an acknowledged review.

Hungry Tomato®
A division of Lerner Publishing Group, Inc.
241 First Avenue North
Minneapolis, MN 55401 USA

For reading levels and more information, look up this title at www.lernerbooks.com.

Main body text set in Billy Serif Regular.

Library of Congress Cataloging-in-Publication Data

Names: Kington, Emily, 1961– author.
Title: I am not a box! / Emily Kington.
Description: Minneapolis : Hungry Tomato, [2019] | Series: Ready-made recycling | Audience: Age 6–9. | Audience: K to Grade 3.
Identifiers: LCCN 2018054310 (print) | LCCN 2018055029 (ebook) | ISBN 9781541555143 (eb pdf) | ISBN 9781541555136 (lb : alk. paper)
Subjects: LCSH: Box craft—Juvenile literature.
Classification: LCC TT870.5 (ebook) | LCC TT870.5 .K375 2019 (print) | DDC 745.5—dc23

LC record available at https://lccn.loc.gov/2018054310

Manufactured in the United States of America
1-45924-42818-1/17/2019